The Healthy Coping Colouring Book and Journal

D0062391

by the same author

Self-Harm and Eating Disorders in Schools
A Guide to Whole-School Strategies and Practical Support
Pooky Knightsmith
Foreword by Sarah Brennan
ISBN 978 1 84905 584 0
eISBN 978 1 78450 031 3

Using Poetry to Promote Talking and Healing
Pooky Knightsmith
Foreword by Catherine Roche and Fiona Pienaar
ISBN 978 1 78592 053 0
eISBN 978 1 78450 323 9

of related interest

The CBT Art Activity Book
100 illustrated handouts for creative therapeutic work
Jennifer Guest
ISBN 978 1 84905 665 6

Stay Cool and In Control with the Keep-Calm Guru
Wise Ways for Children to Regulate their Emotions and Senses
Lauren Brukner
Illustrated by Apsley
ISBN 978 1 78592 714 0

The Healthy Coping Colouring Book and Journal

Creative Activities to Help Manage Stress, Anxiety and Other Big Feelings

Pooky Knightsmith

Illustrated by Emily Hamilton

Jessica Kingsley *Publishers*
London and Philadelphia

First published in 2017
by Jessica Kingsley Publishers
73 Collier Street
London N1 9BE, UK
and
400 Market Street, Suite 400
Philadelphia, PA 19106, USA

www.jkp.com

Library of Congress Cataloging in Publication Data
Names: Knightsmith, Pooky, author.
Title: The healthy coping colouring book and journal : creative activities to help manage stress, anxiety and other big feelings / Pooky Knightsmith and Emily Hamilton.
Description: London ; Philadelphia : Jessica Kingsley Publishers, 2017.
Identifiers: LCCN 2016030807 | ISBN 9781785921391 (alk. paper)
Subjects: LCSH: Art therapy for children--Juvenile literature. | Coloring books--Therapeutic use--Juvenile literature. | Diaries--Authorship--Therapeutic use--Juvenile literature. | Stress management for children--Juvenile literature. | Emotions in children--Juvenile literature.
Classification: LCC RJ505.A7 .K625 2016 | DDC 618.92/891656--dc23

British Library Cataloguing in Publication Data
A CIP catalogue record for this book is available from the British Library

ISBN 978 1 78592 139 1
eISBN 978 1 78450 405 2

Printed and bound in the United States of America

For Lyra and Ellie
The most wonderful daughters in the world

We hope this will be a place where you
can explore and express your feelings.
Make it your own with drawing,
writing and colour – have fun!
We've included loads of ideas to help you
manage on more difficult days, as well as
plenty of uplifting quotes and poems.

We hope you enjoy making your journal
your own as much as we enjoyed creating it!

Pooky & Emily

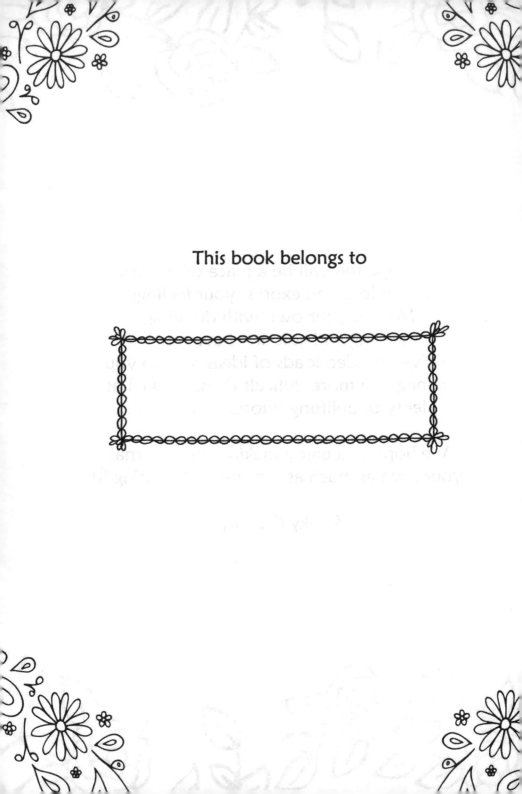

This book belongs to

Date _____

I'm feeling _____

Because _____
_____
_____
_____
_____
_____
_____
_____
_____
_____
_____
_____
_____
_____

MY PICTURE TO REPRESENT HAPPINESS... ☀

Let your imagination roam...you can draw something or someone, or something more abstract like a pattern. Think about using colours that make you happy too...

HAPPY SPECTRUM

I feel:

1   2   3   4   5   6   7   8   9   10

VERY UNHAPPY ☹   ☺ VERY HAPPY

I could move up one by:

_____

_____

_____

_____

_____

_____

_____

_____

Venting BIG Feelings

SOMETIMES OUR FEELINGS BECOME TOO MUCH FOR US TO BEAR. THESE IDEAS ARE ALL DESIGNED TO HELP YOU FEEL BETTER AT THOSE TIMES

- PUNCH A PUNCHBAG OR PILLOW
- SING LOUDLY
- TEAR UP AN OLD MAGAZINE
- RUN REALLY, REALLY FAST
- WRITE OR DRAW WHAT'S UPSET YOU THEN DESTROY IT

YOUR IDEAS HERE:

TAKE TIME FOR FRIENDS

Take time to talk,

Take time to care,

Take time to tell your friend you're there

Take time to pause,

Take time to hear,

Take time to tell your friend you're near.

Take time to laugh,

Take time to pry,

Take time to hold your friend and cry.

Take time to be a real friend,
It's the most precious time you'll spend.

Date _____

I'm feeling _____

Because _____

The best
way to
hold on...
is to
let go.

Time to Talk

Speak for she is listening,
Today, you will be heard.
With open ears,
And open heart,
She'll hear your every word.

And if the words feel broken,
Well, that's okay as well.
You can cry,
And hold her hand,
Until it's time to tell.

The hardest words don't come fast,
You may falter, you may fall,
But carry on,
Say every word,
She'll listen to them all.

And once those words are out there,
Not imprisoned in your head,
That burden
You have held alone,
Will now be shared instead.

Support and advice

Your worries always feel bigger when you keep them to yourself. The longer you keep them to yourself the bigger they grow.

Who could you talk to about something that worried you?

Date _____

I'm feeling _____

Because _____

_____

_____

_____

_____

_____

_____

_____

_____

_____

_____

_____

_____

_____

_____

Painting your feelings

Sometimes BIG feelings need to be expressed in a BIG way.

A fun idea that can help us to express BIG feelings is to use a huge piece of paper and have fun with colour.

Sweeping strokes,
Splashes and splatters of colour,
Footprints, handprints

Whatever you like! No one else needs to see it unless you want them to.

Try using colours that represent how you feel now or how you want to try to feel.

Date _____

I'm feeling _____

Because _____

You are not a
drop in the ocean,
but an ocean
in a drop

"Cracks in concrete serve as proof that even when you are strong, you can fail."

Date _____

I'm feeling _____

Because _____

_____

_____

_____

_____

_____

_____

_____

_____

_____

_____

_____

_____

_____

_____

_____

_____

_____

_____

_____

_____

EVERY SUCCESS
STARTS WITH
A DECISION
TO TRY

'Small things become great things
when done with love'

When you're feeling down or alone

THESE ARE IDEAS WHICH MIGHT HELP YOU
IF YOU FEEL ALONE OR SAD:

- LOOK AT PHOTOGRAPHS OF FRIENDS AND FAMILY
- TELL SOMEONE ABOUT YOUR BEST DAY EVER
- CALL A HELPLINE OR USE AN ONLINE FORUM
- LISTEN TO A SONG THAT REMINDS YOU OF A HAPPY TIME
- GO TO THE PARK AND SWING, LISTEN TO
  THE LAUGHTER OF CHILDREN PLAYING
- RE-READ A FAVOURITE CHILDHOOD BOOK

The importance of sleep

Getting enough sleep is really important for keeping both our minds and bodies healthy, but most people don't get enough sleep.

Simple things you can do to help yourself get more sleep include:

- Going to bed at the same time each night
- Doing calm activities just before bed
- Not using a screen in bed
- Avoiding tea and coffee in the run up to bedtime

Can't sleep?

TRY THESE IDEAS...

Z

Z

Z

Z

Z

Z

Z

- Listening to calming music
- Counting slowly in your head
- Focusing on relaxed breathing

If you still can't get to sleep, try doing something calming like reading or colouring before trying to sleep again.

Z

Z

Z

Z

"A good life should always be made, not waited for."

GET ACTIVE!

A great way of managing our feelings is to get active. There are loads of different ways of doing this. You could:

- Play your favourite sport

- Dance like nobody is watching

- Jump around (trampolines are great stress busters)

- Run!

- Do gymnastics

- Go for a swim

- Walk, alone or with a friend

Date _____

I'm feeling _____

_____

Because _____

_____

_____

_____

_____

_____

_____

_____

_____

_____

_____

_____

_____

_____

_____

_____

_____

_____

Date _____

I'm feeling _____
_____

Because _____
_____
_____
_____
_____
_____
_____
_____
_____
_____
_____
_____
_____
_____
_____
_____
_____
_____
_____
_____

Worried about a friend?

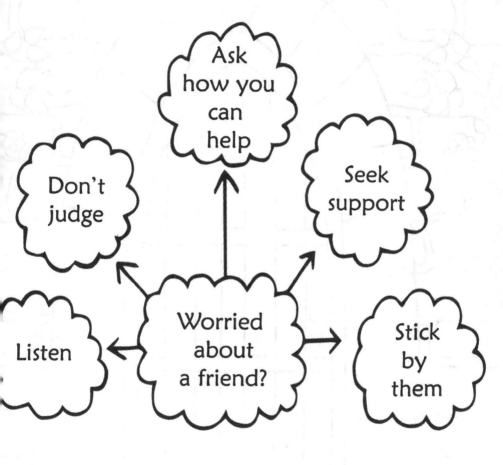

"ALL IS WELL THAT ENDS WELL...
AND IF IT IS NOT WELL,
IT'S NOT THE END...
THE STORY IS NOT YET OVER,
MY FRIEND"

"I HOPE YOU KNOW YOU'RE
CAPABLE,
BRAVE
AND SIGNIFICANT
(EVEN WHEN YOU FEEL
LIKE YOU'RE NOT)"

9 things that can calm a worried mind

1. WRITING IT DOWN

2. TALKING TO SOMEONE

3. GOING FOR A WALK

4. LISTENING TO HAPPY MUSIC

5. A CUP OF TEA

6. A GOOD CRY

7. DRAWING OR COLOURING

8. YOUR IDEA HERE

9. YOUR IDEA HERE

Date _____

I'm feeling _____

Because _____

Date _____

I'm feeling _____

Because _____

_____

_____

_____

_____

_____

_____

_____

_____

_____

_____

_____

Cat Therapy

She guides me well
This cat of mine
She soon can tell
When I'm not fine
And then you'll find her
By my side
My ever faithful
Purring guide

My happy playlist

Music can be a great way to lift your mood when you are feeling down. What songs help you to find your happy?

A SONG THAT ALWAYS MAKES ME SMILE:

_____

A SONG THAT MAKES ME WANT TO DANCE:

_____

A SONG THAT REMINDS ME OF HAPPY TIMES:

_____

A SONG I LOVE TO SING TO:

_____

When you feel down, try listening to these songs and write or draw about how they made you feel.

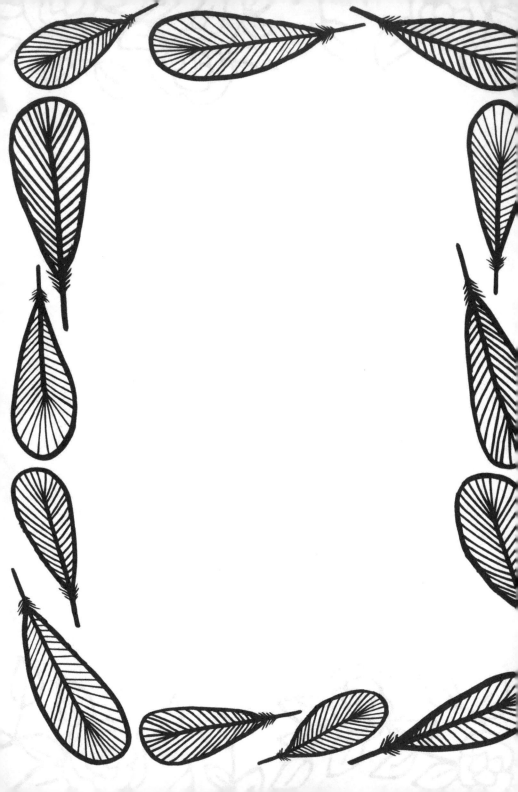

Date _____

I'm feeling _____
_____

Because _____
_____
_____
_____
_____
_____
_____
_____
_____
_____
_____
_____
_____
_____
_____
_____

almost Special

Almost, but not quite special,
Was how he thought he was,
He was very nearly handsome,
But he wasn't quite, because
His ears were slightly pointy,
His nose a bit too long
And the colour of his skin
Was altogether slightly wrong.
He was very nearly clever,
In every class he did quite well,
But he hadn't found a subject yet,
In which he could excel.
He was very almost popular,
He had a lot of friends,
Well maybe they weren't friends as such
Just boys with time to spend.
So he thought he wasn't special,
Very nearly, but not quite;
But this mix of 'not quite special'
Made a boy who was just right.

Date _____

I'm feeling _____
_____

Because _____
_____
_____
_____
_____
_____
_____
_____
_____
_____
_____
_____
_____
_____

Bright Light Shining

The stars above look fuzzy;
Little un-neat pools of light.
They are lacking definition,
But they always shine so bright.

They look like spots of magic,
Floating far off in the sky,
Shining bright light down upon us,
Leaking comfort when we cry.

And their lack of definition,
Is because you can't define
The power of a guiding light
That's with you over time.

A happy memory

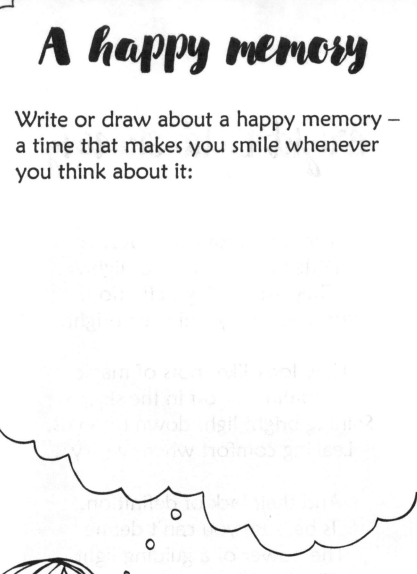

Write or draw about a happy memory – a time that makes you smile whenever you think about it:

Next time you feel down, why not tr·
- Revisiting this memory in your mind
- Writing or drawing about this memc
- Telling a friend or trusted adult abou
  this memory
- Recreating this memory and enjoyin
  it again

WE WERE NOT BORN
TO REPEAT HISTORY
BUT WE WERE BORN
TO MAKE HISTORY

Date _____

I'm feeling _____

Because _____

_____

_____

_____

_____

_____

_____

_____

_____

_____

_____

_____

_____

HEALTHY COPING - DISTRACTIONS

If you've got horrible thoughts or feelings going round and round in your head, one of these distractions might help:

- Call a friend
- Do a jigsaw
- Read
- Watch your favourite TV show
- Look for pictures in the clouds
- Tidy and organise your room
- Go for a walk
- Do some exercise

Date _____

I'm feeling _____

Because _____

Smiles

Smiles are a precious gift,
More precious when they're few.
I know that I don't smile a lot,
So if I smile at you
Please take my smile
And treasure it
And smile back in return,
I know that real smiles are scarce
And sometimes hard to earn.
So if I see a real smile
Play across your face,
I'll wrap it tight around me
And accept it with good grace.

Date _____

I'm feeling _____

Because _____

"People who judge
don't matter.
It's the people who matter
that don't judge."

PUTTING YOUR WORRIES ON PAPER

If something is worrying you, it can really help to put it down on paper instead of letting it go round and round in your head.

Write or draw what you're worried about – don't worry about getting it perfect, just get it OUT.

You could:

Share it
Show it to someone you trust to help them understand how you feel

Destroy it
Tear it up – this can help you vent feelings if you're sad or angry

Save it
Put it somewhere safe and add to it if you feel the need to

Date _____

I'm feeling _____

Because _____

_____

_____

_____

_____

_____

_____

_____

_____

_____

_____

_____

_____

_____

_____

_____

_____

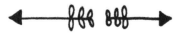

"THE THOUGHTS IN YOUR HEAD
ARE NOT ALWAYS CORRECT.

DO NOT ALWAYS BELIEVE THEM.

ESPECIALLY THE NEGATIVE ONES"

Asking for help

If you're finding things difficult and you want the help of a trusted adult (maybe a parent or teacher) it can feel a bit scary having the first conversation.

Here are some tips to help you:

- Write a list of what you want to say
- Practice saying it aloud
- Make sure you won't be disturbed – you could say 'I want to talk to you about something important, please can we talk privately?'
- Take it slowly – take as long as you need to
- It's okay to cry
- Accept the help that's offered

My notes:

BE BRAVE,
PROBLEMS FEEL SMALLER ONCE WE'VE SHARED THEM

Date _____

I'm feeling _____

Because _____

"LIFE IS LIKE A CAMERA...
FOCUS ON WHAT'S IMPORTANT.
CAPTURE THE GOOD TIMES,
DEVELOP FROM THE NEGATIVES,
AND IF THINGS DON'T WORK OUT,
TAKE ANOTHER SHOT."

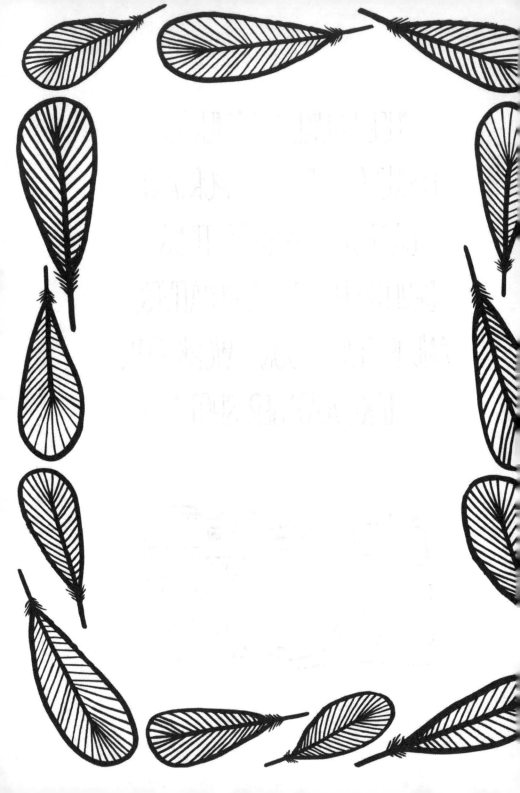

Feeling in control

Sometimes it feels like everything is out of control. Here are some ideas that can help you to feel calmer and more in control of things:

- Put your books in height, alphabetical or colour order
- Build something intricate like a toy brick model
- Paint by numbers
- Read a kids' 'choose your own adventure' book and make all the 'wrong' choices
- Make bread from scratch
- Give your bedroom a facelift by shifting the furniture around
- Give your room a deep clean

Date _____

I'm feeling _____

Because _____

_____

_____

_____

_____

_____

_____

_____

_____

_____

_____

_____

_____

_____

_____

Date _____

I'm feeling _____

Because _____

_____

_____

_____

_____

_____

_____

_____

_____

_____

_____

_____

_____

_____

How To be a good listener

One of the most important jobs we do as friends is to listen to each other.
Here are some ideas about how to be a great listener when your friends need to talk:

- Just listen – stop everything else
- Talk less – your friend should do the talking, not you
- Don't judge – just listen and try to understand
- Don't guess – let your friend tell their story
- Ask questions – to help your friend explain

If you are concerned about your friend, think together about whether there is a parent, teacher or other adult you could ask for help.

Date _____

I'm feeling _____
_____

Because _____
_____
_____
_____
_____
_____
_____
_____
_____
_____
_____
_____
_____
_____
_____
_____

A problem shared is a problem halved

When we keep our problems to ourselves,

they GROW.

When we share problems, they SHRINK.

Date _____

I'm feeling _____

Because _____

Sing, sing, sing!

A fun way to make yourself feel good is to put your favourite music on loud and sing, sing, sing

You could try it in the shower

Who cares if you're in tune, just have fun!

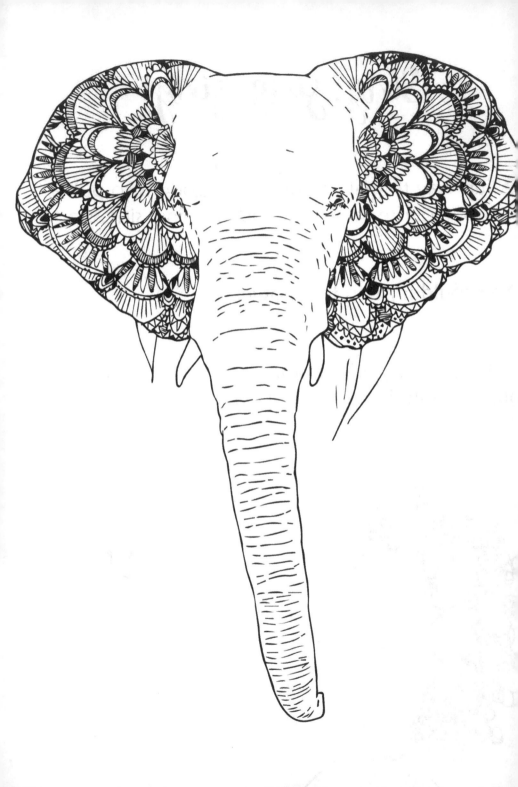

MY ANGRY LIST

List 5 things that make you angry and write or draw about them:

1.

2.

3.

4.

5.

Which one makes you most angry? Number ___

Why?

Why not try talking to someone you trust about it and seeing if, between you, you can think of ways to make it better?

Things I could try:

Eat well

Food is the fuel we need to keep our bodies and minds healthy.

Small changes can make a BIG difference. Do you:

- Make time for breakfast every day?

- Eat plenty of fruit and vegetables?

- Eat well at meal times instead of filling up on snacks?

- Share meal times with friends or family?

- Try new foods?

- Eat sugary snacks and drinks only occasionally?

- Enjoy your food?

Sleeping Space

If you have your own room or space
you can retreat to, there are a few
things you can do to make it an easier
place to sleep and relax:

Having a comfortable bed and bedding
that makes you feel safe and snuggly

Keeping your room neither
too hot nor too cold

Making your room dark at
night, but letting light and
fresh air in during the day

Doing busy activities elsewhere.
If we do highly active or stressful
things in our room, it can stop
us feeling like it is a place to
rest and relax

"WHEN LIFE GIVES YOU LEMONS,
MAKE ORANGE JUICE.
THINK OUTSIDE THE BOX."

Feeling confused?

SOMETIMES OUR HEAD IS A JUMBLE OF CONFUSED FEELINGS. THESE IDEAS CAN HELP US TO GET TO THE BOTTOM OF THINGS.

- WRITE A POEM CALLED 'I DON'T UNDERSTAND'
- PAINT A BIG, ABSTRACT, PICTURE USING POSTER PAINTS
- WRITE DOWN ALL THE QUESTIONS IN YOUR HEAD
- STOP AND WORK BACKWARDS THROUGH THE LAST HOUR TRYING TO ANSWER THE QUESTION 'WHAT MADE ME FEEL THIS WAY?'
- LISTEN TO OR PLAY MUSIC THAT SOUNDS LIKE HOW YOU FEEL

Date _____

I'm feeling _____

Because _____

_____

_____

_____

_____

_____

_____

_____

_____

_____

_____

_____

_____

_____

_____

_____

_____

_____

_____

Date _____

I'm feeling _____
_____

Because _____
_____
_____
_____
_____
_____
_____
_____
_____
_____
_____
_____
_____
_____
_____

The kind things people say

Keep a note here of kind things people say to or about you – it's nice to remember the good things and it can feel good to read them back if you ever doubt yourself.

Nobody can go back
and make a
new beginning
but anyone can
start today and
make a new ending

Relaxation: Box Breathing

When BIG feelings overcome us, controlling our breathing can help us feel better, fast. Box breathing is a simple idea you might find helpful.

1. Breathe in slowly whilst you count to ten.

2. Hold your breath for a count of ten.

3. Breathe out slowly whilst you count to ten.

4. Hold your lungs empty for a count of ten.

5. Repeat.

Practise this a few times when you feel perfectly calm, then you'll be ready to use it when you really need it.

Date _____

I'm feeling _____

Because _____

"Don't become so focused on the finish line that you forget to enjoy the journey"

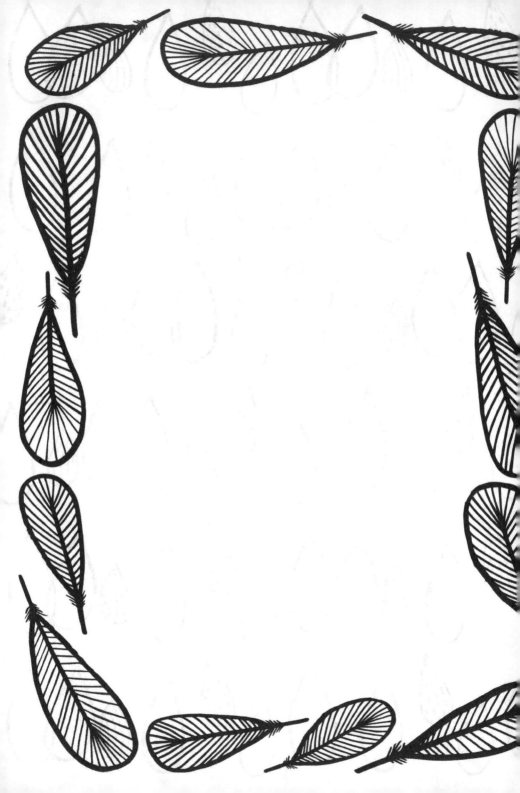

Feeling sad

It's okay to feel sad sometimes – we shouldn't feel scared of this feeling or try to hide it. It can help to seek comfort in things which help us feel a little better. Here are some ideas to try:

- Talk to someone

- Pet an animal

- Listen to a favourite song

- Write

- Paint

- Walk

- Cuddle

- Cry

- Add a few of your own:

Date

I'm feeling

Because

Date _____

I'm feeling _____

Because _____

"WE ARE ALL WONDERFUL,
BEAUTIFUL WRECKS.
THAT'S WHAT CONNECTS US -
THAT WE'RE ALL
BEAUTIFULLY IMPERFECT."

Date _____

I'm feeling _____

_____

Because _____

_____

_____

_____

_____

_____

_____

_____

_____

_____

_____

_____

_____

_____

_____

_____

_____

_____

_____

_____

Sharing your worries

When we experience difficult feelings
like sadness, loneliness, worry or fear,
it can help to talk to someone we trust.

Who could you talk to:

A friend:

Good to talk to when:

Because:

An adult I trust at school or at a club:

Good to talk to when:

Because:

An adult I trust at home / outside school:

Good to talk to when:

Because:

Date _____

I'm feeling _____

Because _____

_____

_____

_____

_____

_____

_____

_____

_____

_____

_____

_____

_____

_____

_____

_____

"THERE'S NO NEED
TO BE PERFECT
TO INSPIRE OTHERS.
LET OTHERS BE INSPIRED
BY HOW YOU MANAGE
YOUR IMPERFECTIONS"

Date _____

I'm feeling _____

_____

Because _____

_____

_____

_____

_____

_____

_____

_____

_____

_____

_____

_____

_____

_____

_____

_____

_____

_____

_____

Angry Monster

Draw or write about a monster that represents everything to do with feeling angry.

Things that make the angry monster grow bigger and more fierce:

Things that help me tame the angry monster:

Sad Monster

Draw or write about a monster that represents everything to do with feeling sad.

- Things that make the sad monster grow bigger and sadder:

- Things that help the sad monster feel happier

Date _____

I'm feeling _____

Because _____

_____

_____

_____

_____

_____

_____

_____

_____

_____

_____

_____

_____

_____

_____

_____

_____

One minute at a time...

IF THINGS FEEL BAD, TRY MANAGING THEM ONE MINUTE AT A TIME.

BEFORE
I FEEL:

TERRIBLE ☐----------------☐ WONDERFUL

ONE MINUTE
NOW I FEEL:

TERRIBLE ☐----------------☐ WONDERFUL

TRY ANOTHER MINUTE
NOW I FEEL:

TERRIBLE ☐----------------☐ WONDERFUL

KEEP GOING AS LONG AS YOU NEED TO.

Storm in a Teacup

Rain drops on a window pane,
Tears in a well,
Rivers bursting river banks
That can't contain the swell.
Things are running riot,
But all colour's leeched and grey;
It's a swirling. whirling maelstrom
In a teacup
Kind of day.

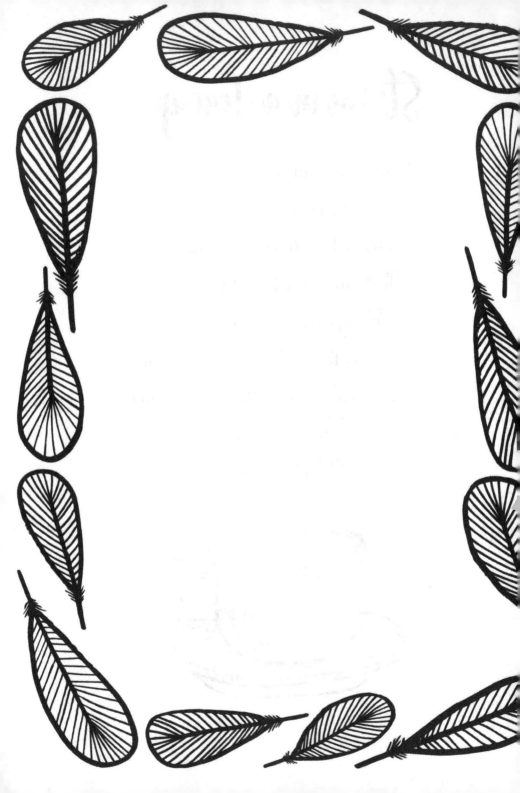

"CHALLENGES ARE NOT
STUMBLING BLOCKS,
THEY ARE BUILDING BLOCKS
FOR CONSTRUCTING
OUR DREAMS"

Date

I'm feeling

Because

"Why stop dreaming when you wake up?"

Fly away

If I had wings
I'd fly away
And leave the world behind.
I'd fly so fast
The thoughts I have
Would empty from my mind.
I'd loop and turn
And dive and spin
And twist in circles high,
And feel the wind
Beneath my wings
In a blue and cloudless sky.
If I had wings
The world would shrink
As I flew far away,
And left my problems far behind
To face another day.

Date _____

I'm feeling _____

Because _____
_____
_____
_____
_____
_____
_____
_____
_____
_____
_____
_____
_____
_____
_____
_____
_____
_____
_____
_____

Date _____

I'm feeling _____

Because _____

_____

_____

_____

_____

_____

_____

_____

_____

_____

_____

_____

_____

_____

_____

Words that inspire me

Make a record of your favourite quotes that inspire you here:

They might come from books or films, friends of family, their source doesn't matter – what matters is that when you read these words, they make you feel GOOD.

"Learn from yesterday

Live for today

Hope for tomorrow"

Date _____

I'm feeling _____

Because _____

A day with friends

With drooping eyelids,
She took herself to bed,
To think back over
What had been done and said.
Of fun times had
Of smiles shared
Of friends who came
And hugged and cared.
As sleep arrived,
Her smile was sweet.
This day with friends
Had been a treat.

Date _____

I'm feeling _____

Because _____
_____
_____
_____
_____
_____
_____
_____
_____
_____
_____
_____
_____
_____
_____
_____
_____
_____
_____

"Make someone smile.
You might not change
the whole world, but you'll
change their world."

Healthy Coping in busy situations

Here are a few ideas that can help you manage difficult feelings in difficult situations without anyone even noticing:

- Scream in your head.
- Imagine yourself in a safe place.
- Become aware of every part of your body in turn: think about your toes, then your ankles, then your knees, etc.
- Breathe deeply whilst counting to five.
- If you're amongst strangers, pick one and imagine what they did last Friday.

Date

I'm feeling

Because

Date _____

I'm feeling _____

Because _____

"Not to spoil
the end For you,
but everything
is going to be
okay"

Kind words
can be short
and Easy to speak
but their echoes
are endless

Date _____

I'm feeling _____
_____

Because _____
_____
_____
_____
_____
_____
_____
_____
_____
_____
_____
_____
_____
_____
_____
_____

Someone who inspires me

Who inspires you? You could either choose someone famous or someone you know in real life.

I am inspired by:

Because:

I could be more like them by:

Happy Hobbies

Hobbies can be a great way to make you feel good. Having an activity that you do purely for fun can help you to relax and free your mind from any worries you might have.

Hobbies that other people have found helpful include:

Reading
Writing
Painting
Knitting
Sewing
Football
Hockey
Netball
Dancing
Gymnastics
Playing an instrument
Watching films
Horse riding
Dog walking

Best books ever...

Reading can be a great way to lift our mood or inspire us. Think about your favourite books and list them below.

Why not re-read one of them and encourage a friend to read it too so you can enjoy the story together?

My favourite books:

1.
Because:

2.
Because:

3.
Because:

4.
Because:

A book I haven't read yet but would love to:

Date _____

I'm feeling _____
_____

Because _____
_____
_____
_____
_____
_____
_____
_____
_____
_____
_____
_____
_____
_____
_____

"SOMETIMES WHEN
YOU'RE IN A DARK PLACE
AND YOU THINK YOU'VE BEEN BURIED,
YOU'VE ACTUALLY
BEEN PLANTED."

Date _____

I'm feeling _____

Because _____

_____

_____

_____

_____

_____

_____

_____

_____

_____

_____

_____

_____

_____

_____

_____

_____

"A GOOD FRIEND IS SOMEONE
WHO THINKS YOU'RE A GOOD EGG
EVEN THOUGH THEY KNOW
YOU'RE SLIGHTLY CRACKED"

Date _____

I'm feeling _____

Because _____

_____

_____

_____

_____

_____

_____

_____

_____

_____

_____

_____

_____

_____

_____

Date _____

I'm feeling _____
_____

Because _____
_____
_____
_____
_____
_____
_____
_____
_____
_____
_____
_____
_____
_____
_____
_____

Date _____

I'm feeling _____

Because _____

Cloud spotting

If you find yourself feeling sad,
angry or otherwise overwhelmed
and you need to calm down,
cloud spotting can work well.
Head outside or find a window
and see what shapes you can
spot in the clouds.

Tip: if it's a completely clear day,
look for patterns in tree trunks or
floor tiles.

Date _____

I'm feeling _____
_____

Because _____
_____
_____
_____
_____
_____
_____
_____
_____
_____
_____
_____
_____
_____
_____
_____
_____

Feed the birds

Watching birds can be very calming. If you have a garden or window sill, try setting up a bird feeder or small plate of bird seed. After a few days, birds will visit regularly and provide a calming distraction.

See how many different types of birds you can learn to recognise.

If there is nowhere you can leave food for the birds, is there somewhere you could go to watch birds in the woods or to feed ducks at a pond?

Date _____

I'm feeling _____

Because _____

_____

_____

_____

_____

_____

_____

_____

_____

_____

_____

_____

_____

_____

_____

_____

_____

"Courage doesn't always roar.
Sometimes courage is
the quiet voice at the
end of the day saying
'I will try again tomorrow'."

Observer

The cat sat
Watching
The world pass by.
She watched as people
Laughed
And cried.
She watched,
And twitched her tail
In time
With the busy
People
Pantomime.
Some stopped
And said hello
To her,
Or stroked her
Ginger,
Silky fur.
But others simply
Walked on past
Some sad and slow,
Some bright and fast.

Healthy Coping: Self-Soothe box

At difficult times, a self-soothe box can be brilliant. This is a box full of things designed to calm you down or distract you until you feel better.

Making one is easy:

1. Find or buy a box and decorate it to your liking
2. Fill the box with things that make you feel good like:
    - Photographs or letters
    - Inspirational quotes
    - A magazine
    - A favourite book
    - A favourite hobby or craft activity
    - Something that tastes goood
    - Something that smells lovely
    - Bubble bath or shower gel
    - A list of music you could listen to
    - This book!

Keep the box somewhere safe and open it up any time you need them. Add or remove things depending on what works.

Date _____

I'm feeling _____

Because _____

Date _____

I'm feeling _____

Because _____

"It always seems impossible until it's done"

Date _____

I'm feeling _____

Because _____

Happy!

Draw or write about things that make you feel happy or good:

Date _____

I'm feeling _____

Because _____

"You can never cross the ocean
unless you have the courage
to lose sight of the shore"

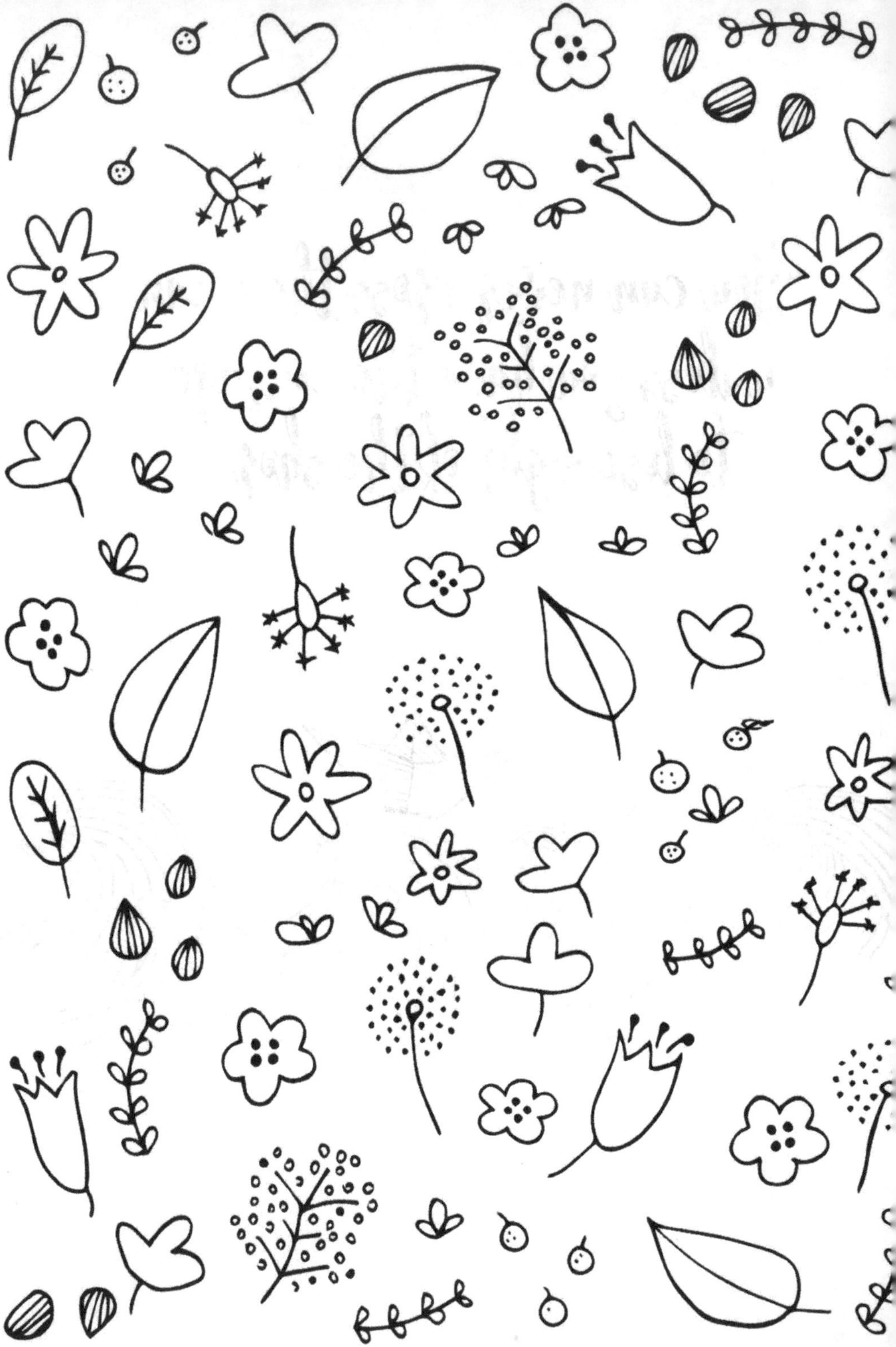

Good luck!

We hope you found some ideas in here that
helped you to find your happy on a sad day.
If you found any of the ideas helpful, please share
them with your friends so they can try them too.

Tell us what you liked and didn't like by writing to

pooky@inourhands.com

You can also tweet us @PookyH

We would love to see some pictures of your
pages all coloured in and written over.

Good luck!

Love Pooky and Emily
xxx